Written by Judy Leimbach and Sharon Eckert Illustrated by Mary Lou Johnson

NEW YORK AND LONDON

First published in 2008 by Prufrock Press Inc.

Published 2021 by Routledge
605 Third Avenue, New York, NY 10017
2 Park Square, Milton Park, Abingdon, Oxon OX14 4RN

Routledge is an imprint of the Taylor & Francis Group, an informa business

ISBN 13: 978-1-5936-3065-2 (pbk)

DOI: 10.4324/9781003234098

Contents

Introduction

Have your students join the Detective Club and work along with the young detectives as they solve the mysteries brought to Shirley, Rita, Quent and Sam by their friends and neighbors. Young students will relate to the everyday problems and will enjoy the challenge these mysteries offer. They will have fun being detectives and will be sharpening their thinking skills in the process.

While solving the mysteries in this book students will gather clues through:

- decoding a message
- sorting information
- solving logic puzzles
- using inferential thinking

In order to reach the correct conclusions, students will use the following skills:

- organizing clues
- combining and analyzing the information presented
- using deductive reasoning
- using the process of elimination.

In this book there are six different scenarios with puzzles for students to solve. Each mystery includes a teacher's guide with complete instructions for the teacher and the answers to the puzzles.

Using a Grid to Solve Logic Puzzles

This introductory section gives students the opportunity to work the puzzles that Sam Smart is required to solve in order to join the Detective Club. Because many of the activities in this book feature matrix logic puzzles, it is important to teach students how to solve this type of puzzle so that they can successfully solve the mysteries that follow. There are six easy puzzles in this section. If your students have not been introduced to matrix logic, you will want to work through the puzzles together until they master the techniques necessary to gather and organize information that is presented in the clues.

The Case of the Mystery Valentine

Anthony receives an unsigned valentine and enlists the help of the Detective Club to determine who sent it. Students must decode a message, sort information, solve two deductive logic puzzles and use inferential thinking to solve the mystery.

The Case of the Lost Backpack

The detectives help Brian and Jessica find the owner of the backpack that was left on the soccer field. To solve the mystery, students need to analyze a variety of information and use the process of elimination.

The Case of the Missing Ribbon

Mrs. Costello calls on the Detective Club when the award ribbon Jimmy's dog won in a dog show disappears from her classroom. In this mystery students will use matrix logic puzzles and analyze information about some of the boys in Jimmy's class to determine who is the most likely person to have taken his ribbon.

The Case of Willie's Wallet

Mr. Corbin calls for help when Willie loses his wallet at the carnival while on a Cub Scout outing. In this mystery students have to gather information about the sequence in which Willie visited different rides and use deductive logic to determine which of his friends found his wallet.

The Case of the Boys Only Club

When Chuck's birthday cake disappears from the "Boys Only" clubhouse, the neighborhood girls are suspects. In this mystery students will use matrix logic puz-

DOI: 10.4324/9781003234098-1

zles to gain information about the six girls. As they find information about each of the girls, they will record it on a chart. Analyzing the information on the chart will lead them to the most likely cake thief. Working through this mystery and recording information on a chart will make it easier to do the last mystery.

The Case of Santa's Gift List

When a strong wind blows Santa's gift list out of his hand while he is delivering gifts on Christmas Eve, he needs some fast help from the Detective Club to get the gifts delivered to the right houses. This mystery is the most difficult in the book. It requires students to solve deductive logic puzzles and sort through a variety of information about five houses and the children who live in them. Unlike the other mysteries, students will not be using grids to sort out the information in the clues. Instead, they will record all the information on a chart. Once all the information is on the chart, they will be able to match each gift with a child. Because clues in the last two puzzles rely on having done the previous puzzles correctly, it would be a good idea to check answers after the first and second puzzles before analyzing the information presented in the last two exercises.

This book is intended to lead young students to discover the excitement of being a detective. Each time they successfully solve a mystery, they will be eager to tackle the next one. Keeping the Detective Log Sheet on page 17 and earning awards such as the certificate on page 64 will add to the excitement and increase your students' feelings of accomplishment. Watch their confidence grow along with their problem solving abilities.

Using a Grid to Solve Logic Puzzles

Teacher's Guide

Most of the mysteries in this book include exercises that require students to get clues by working grid or matrix logic puzzles. If students have not had practice solving logic puzzles using a grid, it is important to give them some instruction and practice. They need to know that:

- A "no" is as important as a "yes" in reaching conclusions.
- Whenever they are able to fill in a "yes," they need to fill in the grid with "nos" both horizontally and vertically. You may choose some other way of marking the grid; for instance, an **X** for "yes" and an **O** for "no."

If the students have not done logic puzzles using a grid, take them step-by-step through the process. The book begins with three activities that are designed to introduce students to solving these puzzles. If your students are familiar with deductive logic puzzles, you can skip this section or have students complete the puzzles independently. Otherwise, you may wish to go through the puzzles together. All three of these introductory exercises contain two puzzles that students must solve before they can get the correct answer.

Most Creative Costume pages 11-12

First Puzzle

In the first puzzle, clue 1 tells us that Kyle's costume was not the headless horseman. Mark a "no" or "O" in that space.

Clue 2 tells us that neither Luke or Kyle was the pirate skeleton. Mark "no" or "O" in those spaces.

If Matt is the pirate skeleton, he cannot be the headless horseman or the alien from space. Mark "no" or "O" in those spaces.

Since Kyle and Matt were not the headless horseman, we can conclude that Luke was. Mark a "yes" or "X" in that space and a "no" or "O" to indicate that Luke was not the alien. This leads to the conclusion that Kyle was the alien.

	Kyle	Luke	Matt
pirate skeleton	O	O	X
alien	X	O	O
headless horseman	O	X	O

Most Creative Costume
First Puzzle

DOI: 10.4324/9781003234098-2

Second Puzzle

In the second puzzle on page 12, clue 1 tells us that the alien did not win the prize for the scariest costume or the most creative costume. Mark "nos" or "Os" in those spaces. This leads us to conclude that the alien won the prize for the funniest costume. Mark "yes" or "X" in that space and "nos" or "Os" to show neither the pirate skeleton nor the headless horseman won the funniest costume prize.

	scariest	funniest	most creative
pirate skeleton	X	O	O
alien	O	X	O
headless horseman	O	O	X

Most Creative Costume
Second Puzzle

Clue 2 tells us that the headless horseman did not win the scariest costume prize. Mark a "no" or "O" in that space. This leads us to conclude that the pirate skeleton won the prize for the scariest costume, and not the most creative. Therefore, the headless horseman must have won the most creative prize.

Answers

Who won? - Luke
What costume? - headless horseman

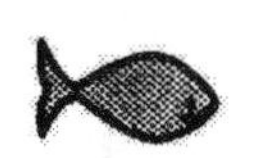

The Biggest Fish, pages 13-14

First Puzzle

In the first puzzle, clue 1 does not tell us who caught the bass, but it does tell us that neither Kim or Bob caught the bass. Mark "nos" or "Os" in those spaces.

	bass	perch	catfish	bluegill
Tom	O	O	O	X
Don	X	O	O	O
Kim	O	O	X	O
Bob	O	X	O	O

The Biggest Fish
First Puzzle

Likewise, clue 2 does not tell us who caught a particular fish, but it does tell us who did not catch a particular fish. Students should fill in the corresponding "nos" or "Os".

Clue 3 tells us that Kim caught the catfish. Students should mark the "yes" or "X" in that space, the "n0" or "O" vertically to show that none of the others caught the catfish, and the "nos" or "Os" horizontally to show that Kim did not catch any other kind of fish.

This will lead students to conclude that Tom caught the bluegill. After marking Tom's catch as a bluegill, putting the "nos" or "Os" horizontally to show that Tom did not catch the other kinds of fish, this will lead to the conclusion that Don caught the bass and Bob caught the perch.

Second Puzzle

Lead students through the second puzzle in the same manner. Direct students to use the conclusion from their logic puzzle grids to answer the questions at the bottom of the page.

Answers:

Who caught the biggest fish? - Kim

What kind of fish was it? - catfish

	8 inches	10 inches	14 inches	20 inches
bass	o	o	x	o
perch	o	x	o	o
catfish	o	o	o	x
bluegill	x	o	o	o

The Biggest Fish
Second Puzzle

Championship Baseball Team, pages 15-16

First Puzzle

In the first puzzle, clue 1 tells us that Greg was not on the Wildcats or the Bears. Read through the other clues with the class and ask what information they can record on their grids from each clue. Instruct them to fill in the grid. Monitor their progress and give help as necessary.

	Tigers	Wildcats	Lions	Bears
Jorge	o	x	o	o
C.J.	o	o	o	x
Steve	o	o	x	o
Greg	x	o	o	o

Championship Baseball Team
First Puzzle

Second Puzzle

Direct students to read the clues for the second puzzle and fill in the grid. Once the grids are complete, they can use the information to answer the questions at the bottom of the page.

Answers:

Which team won? - Lions

Which boy was on that team? - Steve

	1 st	2 nd	3 rd	4 th
Tigers	o	o	x	o
Wildcats	o	x	o	o
Lions	x	o	o	o
Bears	o	o	o	x

Championship Baseball
Second Puzzle

WELCOME TO THE
DETECTIVE CLUB
CLUES

The Detective Club

A New Member

Hi, I'm Shirley Sharp. I am the chief detective at the Detective Club. My friends, Rita Right and Quent Quick, and I have had the detective agency for a year. We are really good at finding lost things. Mostly other kids in the neighborhood come to us for help, but every now and then we get adults who need our help.

One day when we were just sitting around talking about how we had not had a good case in weeks, Rita brought up the idea of bringing a new member into our group.

"There's a new boy in my class," said Rita. "His name is Sam Smart, and he is really smart. I thought he would be good for our group, so I told him about our club. He said he would like to be a detective too. What do you think?"

Quent and I scratched our heads. We were remembering all the other people who had wanted to join our group but just didn't have the skills to be good detectives, like being curious and a good thinker.

After a long pause I suggested, "Why don't we give him a test? We could each make up a short, tricky puzzle that requires logical thinking to solve. If he can solve all three tests, we'll let him be a detective. All in favor, raise your hand."

Quent and Rita's hands shot up into the air. Right away we started making tests for our possible new member.

Most Creative Costume

Rita Right's Test - part 1

At a neighborhood Halloween party, Kyle, Luke, and Matt won prizes for the Halloween costumes they were wearing. Their costumes were a pirate skeleton, an alien from space and a headless horseman. Find out who won the prize for the most creative costume and what costume he was wearing.

Use these clues to find out what costume each person was wearing.

1. Kyle's costume had a head

2. Luke and Kyle walked to the party with the pirate skeleton.

	Kyle	Luke	Matt
pirate skeleton			
alien			
headless horseman			

Most Creative Costume

Rita Right's Test - part 2

At the party prizes were given for the scariest, the funniest and the most creative costumes. Each of the boys won one of the prizes.

Use these clues to discover which prize each costume won.

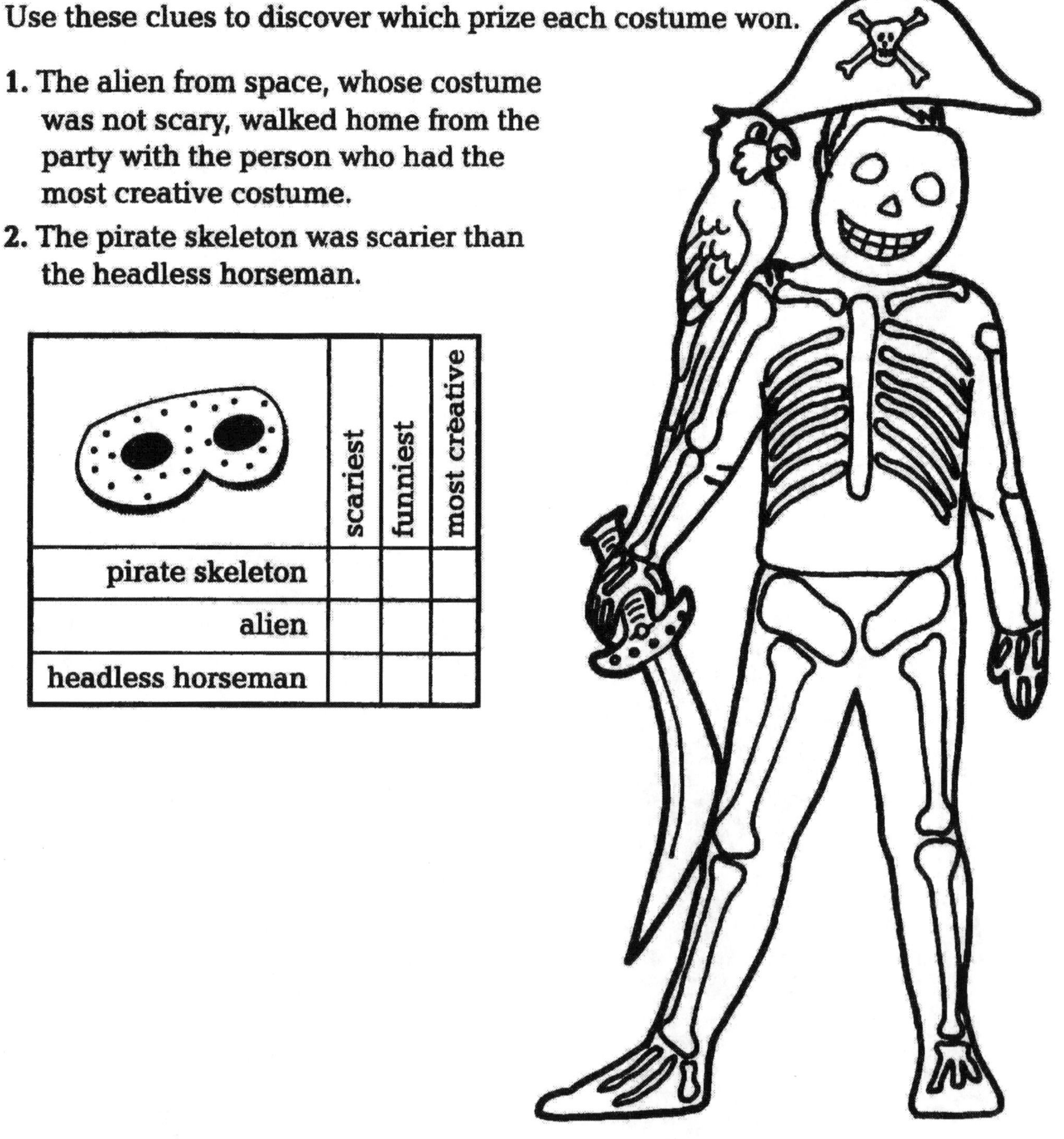

1. The alien from space, whose costume was not scary, walked home from the party with the person who had the most creative costume.
2. The pirate skeleton was scarier than the headless horseman.

	scariest	funniest	most creative
pirate skeleton			
alien			
headless horseman			

Who won the prize for the most creative costume? ________________

What costume was he wearing? ________________

The Biggest Fish

Quent Quick's Test - part 1

One Saturday morning, Tom, Don, Kim and Bob all went fishing together at Hidden Lake. By noon each of them had caught one fish. The fish they caught were a bass, a bluegill, a perch and a catfish. Find out who caught the largest fish and what kind of fish each person caught.

Use these clues to discover which fish each person caught.

1. Tom and Don were fishing together when one of them caught the bass.
2. Tom did not catch the perch, and neither Bob or Don caught the bluegill.
3. The fish Kim caught gets its name from its whiskers.

	bass	perch	catfish	bluegill
Tom				
Don				
Kim				
Bob				

The Biggest Fish

Quent Quick's Test - part 2

Not only did each person catch a different type of fish, but each person caught a fish that was a different length – 8, 10, 14 and 20 inches. Use the following clues to find the length of each fish.

1. The bass was bigger than the bluegill and the perch.
2. The catfish was twice as long as the perch.

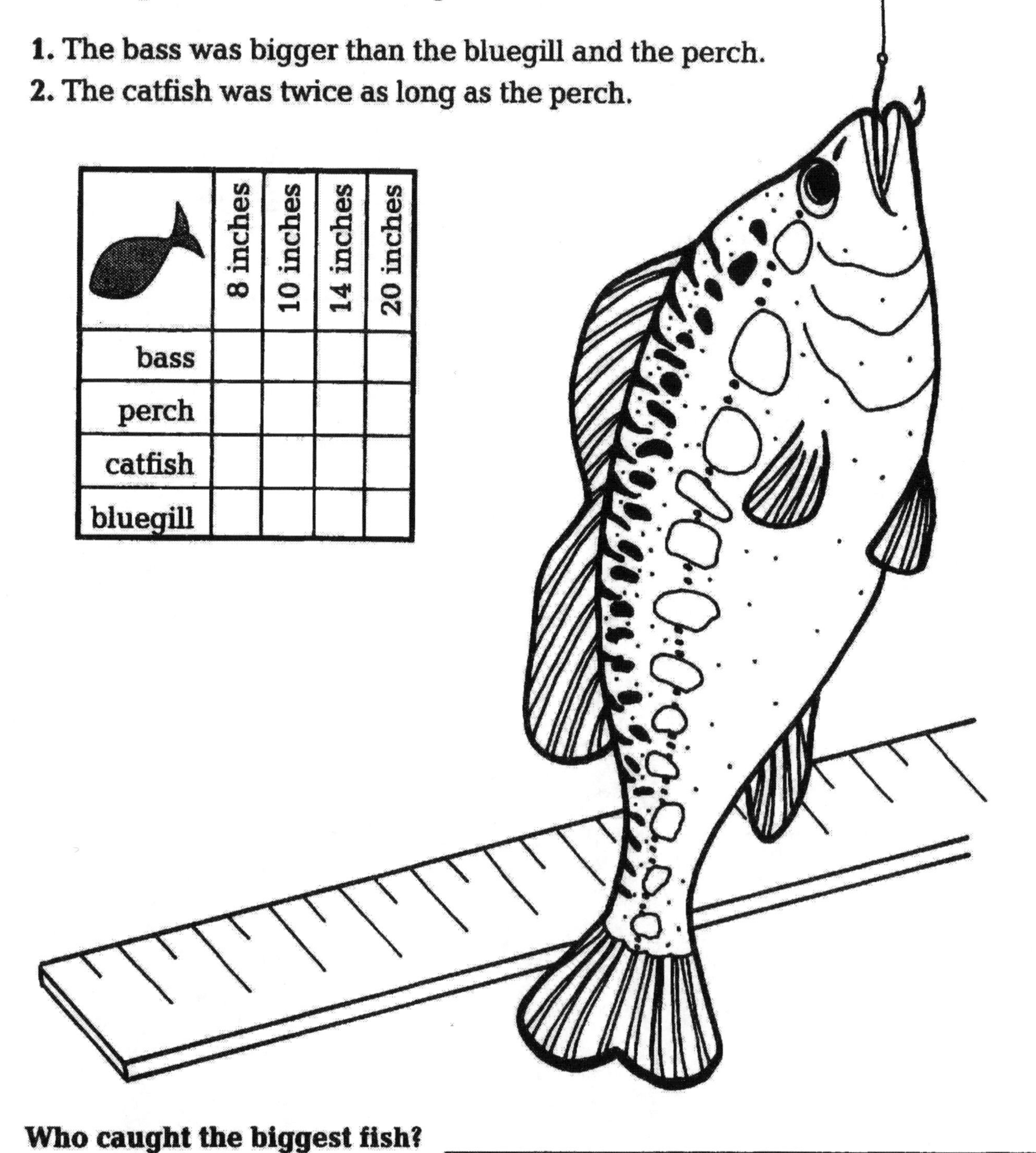

	8 inches	10 inches	14 inches	20 inches
bass				
perch				
catfish				
bluegill				

Who caught the biggest fish? ____________________

What kind of fish was it? ____________________

Championship Baseball Team

Shirley Sharp's Test - part 1

Greg, C.J., Steve, and Jorge were friends who all played on different teams in the Briarcliffe Baseball League. The teams they played on were the Tigers, Wildcats, Lions and Bears. Over the 4th of July weekend, they had their big tournament. Find out which team won the championship and which of the four boys was on the winning team.

Use these clues to find which boy was on each of the teams.

1. Greg's team lost to the Wildcats in the tournament, but they beat the Bears.
2. C.J. and Steve were in the same class as the boy on the Wildcats.
3. Steve was not on the Bears.
4. The boy on the Tigers was not in C.J.'s class

	Tigers	Wildcats	Lions	Bears
Jorge				
C.J.				
Steve				
Greg				

Championship Baseball Team

Shirley Sharp's Test - part 2

Each of the teams won either first, second, third or fourth place in the tournament. Now that you know what team each of the boys played on, use the clues below to find in which place each team finished.

1. The Wildcats did not finish in first place.
2. The Tigers placed ahead of the Bears, but behind the Wildcats and the Lions.

	First	Second	Third	Fourth
Tigers				
Wildcats				
Lions				
Bears				

Which team won the championship? ____________________

Which boy was on the winning team? ____________________

Detective Log Sheet

Detective's Name ______________________

If you were able to solve the puzzles Shirley, Rita and Quent made to test Sam Smart, you are ready to join them in solving some cases. Use this sheet to keep track of all the mysteries you solve.

Name of Case	Date Stated	Date Completed	Case Closed

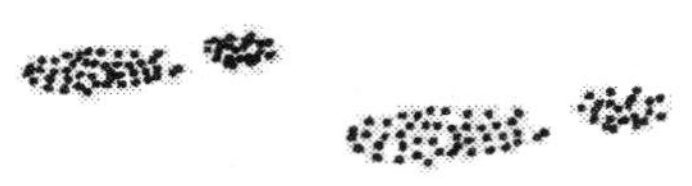

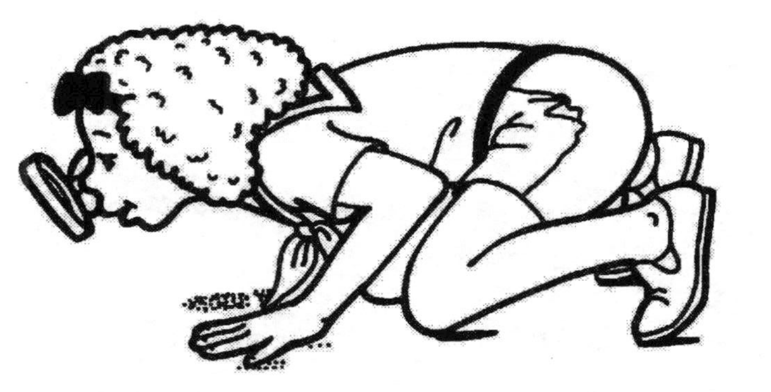

DOI: 10.4324/9781003234098-3

DOI: 10.4324/9781003234098-4

The Mystery Valentine

The Case

Our friend Anthony came to our club house on February 14th with a request to help him figure out who had sent him a mystery valentine. He was really puzzled by one valentine that had not been signed. He explained that it could have been from someone in his class or from someone from the other fourth grade class.

"Rita and I will take this case," I said. "We're better at matters of the heart. First let's get some facts. How many people are in the two classrooms, Anthony?"

"Well," said Anthony, "there are 22 in my class and 23 in Miss Jendryk's class. Plus we each got cards from the teachers. "

"Quick, Quent, help us out. How many valentines did Anthony receive?"

True to his name, Quent shouted out, "That would be 47 valentines."

"But," explained Anthony, "I got 48 valentines."

"Ah-ha," Rita exclaimed. "The plot thickens. An extra valentine. Someone is really trying to throw you off course by giving you a card with his or her name on it and also an unsigned mystery card. We'll need more clues to be able to solve this little mystery."

The Mystery Valentine
A Coded Message

Then Anthony pulled out his valentine and showed us that it had a coded message on the back. Rita and I looked carefully at the message.

"Look at this heart in the bottom corner," Rita pointed out. "This is a clue for sure. Also there is one word with only one letter, the letter, J. The J must stand for either A or I."

"Good thinking Rita." I patted her on the back. "Look at the the number of letters in the signature, the double letters in the first word of the signature, and the question marks after it. I think the HVFTT XIP??? might stand for GUESS WHO???"

Following this logic, we were able to crack the code in no time at all. The coded message said:

___

___

___

___

The Mystery Valentine

A Birthday Clue

"Let's see, Anthony," I said. " The message is inviting you to a birthday party on Saturday. This is an important clue and a great place to start. The person who sent the card must have a birthday in February."

"I know," volunteered Anthony, "Each classroom has a chart of all the January, February and March birthdays in the hall by the door."

The three of us hurried off to school to check out the charts. When we arrived, Mrs. Whitfield's chart was missing. In its place were the following clues.

1. Travis celebrates his birthday when the ground hog looks for its shadow.
2. Soon Lin and Eric have birthdays in the same month, but no one else in their class has birthdays during this month.
3. Holly's birthday is one week before Travis's.
4. Marilyn shares a birthday with Martin Luther King.

?	January	January	February	February	February	February	March	March
Holly								
Travis								
Marilyn								
Rhett								
Soon Lin								
Aaron								
Brook								
Eric								

The Mystery Valentine

Another Birthday Clue

Having narrowed the field of mystery Valentine senders to four people from Mrs. Whitfield's class, we moved across the hall to Miss Jendryk's class. Sure enough, there was a list of clues by that room also. We went to work and quickly had four more February birthdays from her classroom.

1. Tony and Amber were both born on Abraham Lincoln's birthday.

2. Jeff was born on St. Patrick's Day.

3. Larissa's birthday is three weeks before Amber's.

4. Marga's birthday is after Jeff's but before Bao-Chau's.

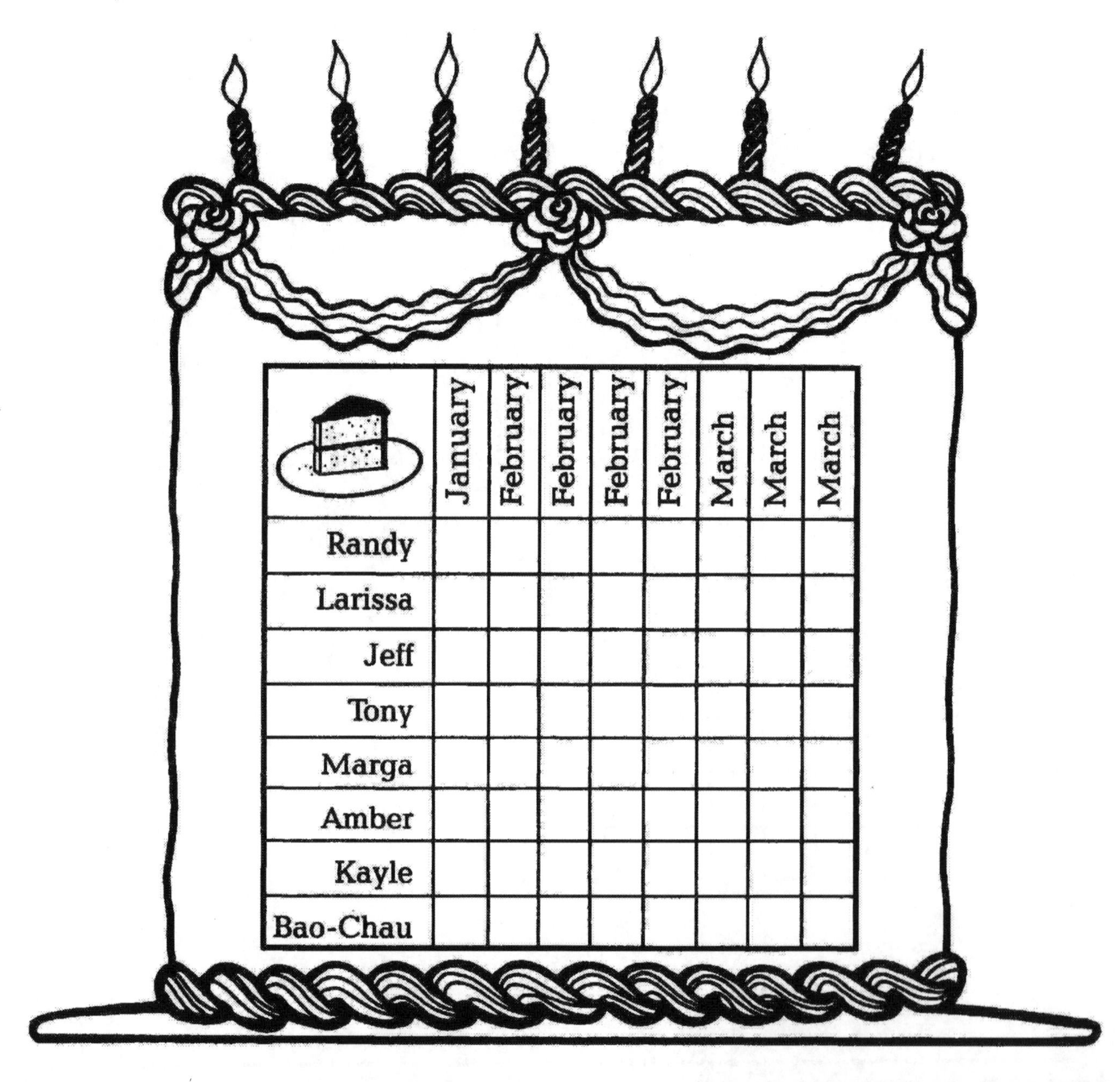

	January	February	February	February	February	March	March	March
Randy								
Larissa								
Jeff								
Tony								
Marga								
Amber								
Kayle								
Bao-Chau								

The Mystery Valentine

Three More Clues

I took out my notebook and listed the first names of the eight students whom we thought might have sent Anthony an invitation to a birthday party. We figured that as we found out more information about any of those students, we could note it next to their names.

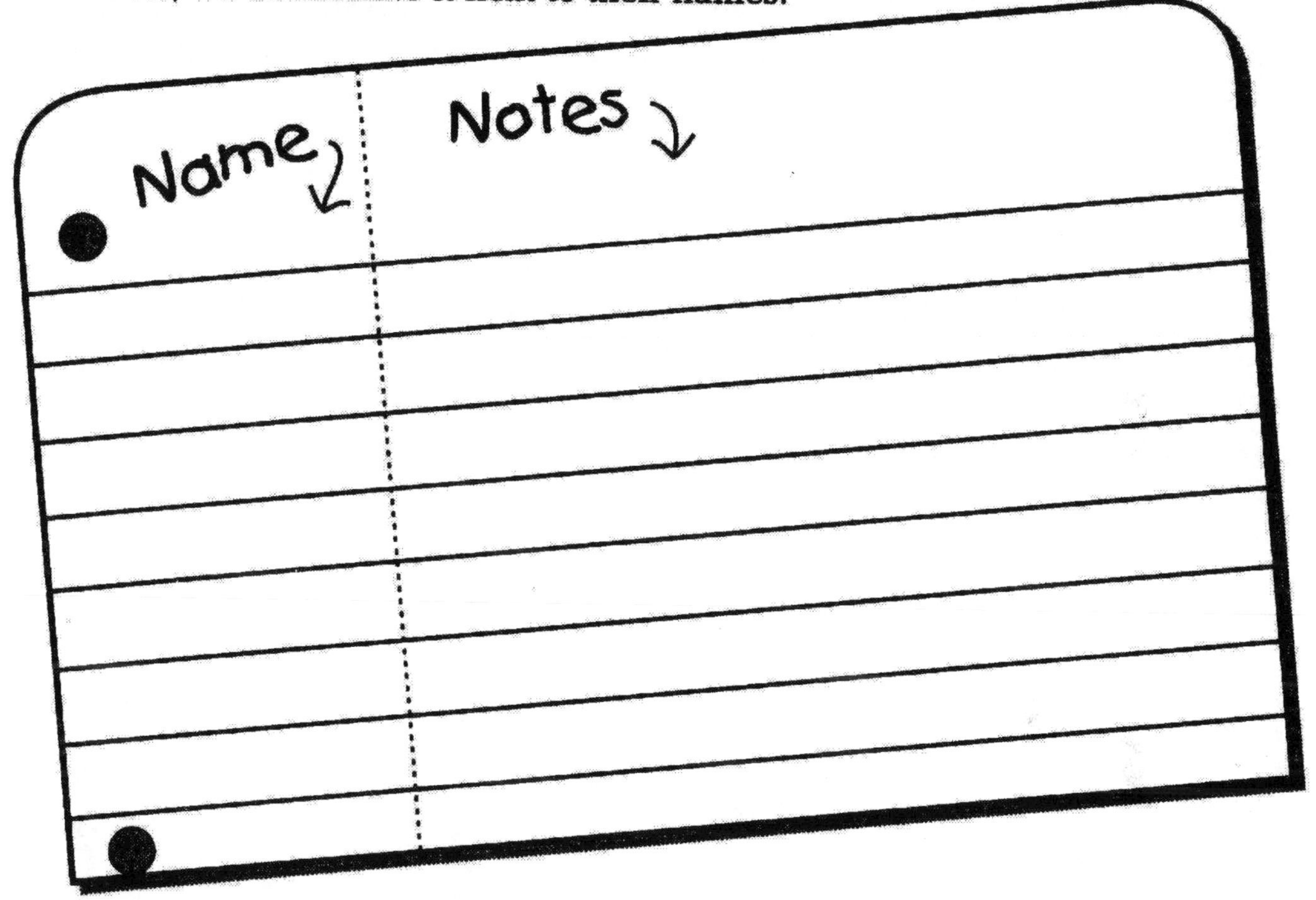

We were really making progress. "Are there any more clues?" we asked.

Anthony took out the mystery valentine's envelope. Rita and I immediately noticed three things:

The envelope was sealed with a valentine sticker.

There was a candy treat taped to the envelope.

There was a chocolate smudge that looked like a fingerprint.

The Mystery Valentine

More Clues and a Conclusion

"Okay, Anthony, what more can you tell us about these eight people?"

Anthony scratched his head and made weird faces for a long time without saying anything. We waited patiently.

Finally he came up with some more clues. As he talked, I recorded the information in my notebook next to each person's name. Here are the final clues.

1. Amber, Kayle, Brook, Travis, and Aaron sealed their valentines with valentine stickers.
2. At treat time Kayle had a chocolate-covered granola bar, Rhett had a chocolate cupcake, Travis had a brownie, and Randy had chocolate-dipped strawberries.
3. Aaron, Brook, Kayle, and Tony taped candy treats to their valentine envelopes.

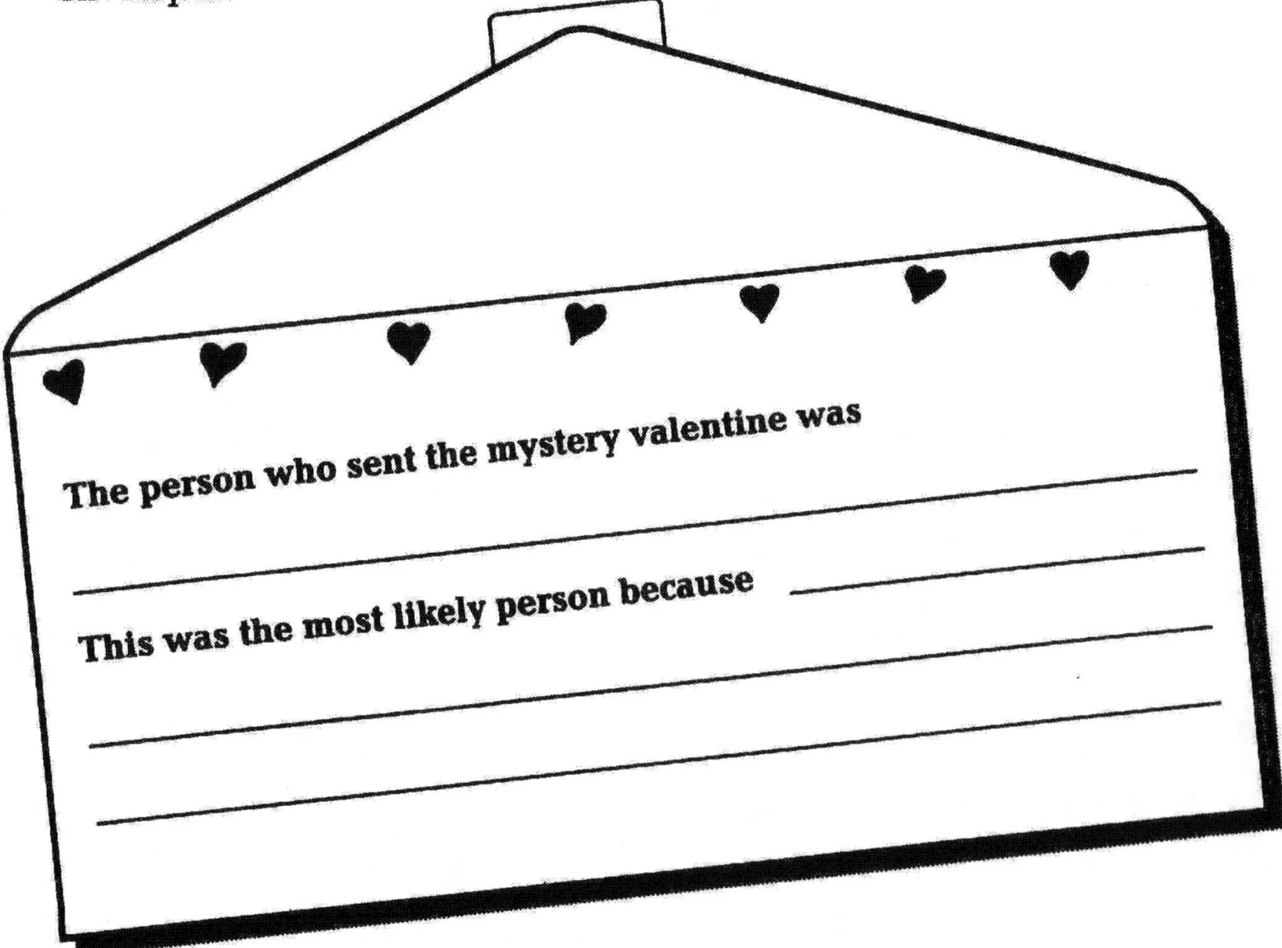

The Mystery Valentine

Teacher's Guide

This mystery presents a situation where someone has received an extra, unsigned valentine. Students must decode a message, sort information, do two deductive logic puzzles, and use inferential thinking to solve the mystery.

1. Introduce the valentine party scenario on page 19. Have students give their ideas about why Anthony has an extra valentine.
2. Direct students to analyze the coded message on the back of the extra valentine as shown on page 20. Have them use Rita's theory and write the letters G-U-E-S-S W-H-O under HVFTT XIP. Seeing that H was used for G, that V was used for U, that F was used for E etc., students should conclude that the code substitutes the next letter in the alphabet for the real letter. Following this pattern, they should be able to decode the message.

   Decoded message:

   You're invited to my birthday party on Saturday if you can guess who I am.
   Guess who?
3. On pages and 21 and 22 students will work two deductive logic puzzles to discover the names of the students with birthdays in February.

   The correct names are:

Travis	Randy
Rhett	Tony
Aaron	Amber
Brook	Kayle
4. Direct students to list the first names of the eight students with February birthdays on the notebook on page 23. Then have them use the information about the envelope on page 24 and the clues on page 24 to solve the mystery. An efficient way to arrive at the answer would be to jot down notes about the people (derived from the clues on page 24) next to the names. For example, they might use "S" next to all who used stickers, "C" next to those who had chocolate, and "T" next to those who taped treats on the envelope. Have them use the information to decide who was the most likely one to have sent the mystery valentine.

Answer: Kayle
1. used stickers to seal her valentines
2. taped a candy treat to the envelopes
3. had chocolate at treat time

DOI: 10.4324/9781003234098-5

The Lost Backpack

The Case

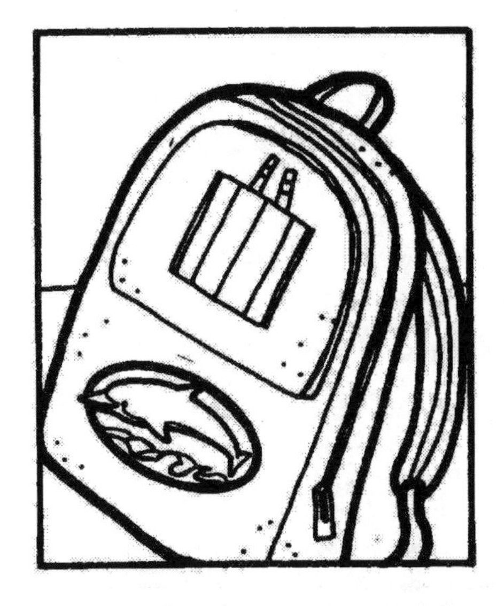

Brian and Jessica came running in one day waving a backpack and shouting, "Detectives, we need your help!"

"Calm down," I said, "and tell us what the problem is."

"Well," started Brian, "someone left this backpack at soccer practice today. Jessica and I were the last ones to leave and we found it. Now we have to find the owner. See, it has a picture of a dolphin and the slogan "Save the Dolphins" on it, but we can't find a name on it."

"Let's do what detectives do best. Let's be snoopy and look inside," said Sam.

Inside we found five books that had been checked out from the school library.

"A clue," offered Sam. "In the summer, the school library is only open to those students who are enrolled in the Super Summer Reading Program."

"Great thinking Sam. You're my partner on this case. Rita and Quent, you stay here and answer the phone."

As we walked out the door Rita called after us, "It must belong to someone who is on their soccer team and also in the Super Summer Reading Program."

Sam and I rolled our eyes at each other. "Elementary, Rita," we sang out together.

The Lost Backpack

Two Lists

We walked down the street pondering our first move. Brian said he had a team roster of all the members of the Silver Streaks. Jessica said her mom worked part-time in the school library so she would have a list of summer readers.

Sam and Brian got the list of the soccer players, and Jessica and I got the names of the people who were enrolled in the summer reading program. We met at Jessica's house. Now all we had to do was compare the lists.

Silver Streaks Soccer

Lance Barker *(643-5063)*
Damon Burns *(643-3785)*
Rose Demont *(643-3123)*
Eric Gillespie *(643-2728)*
Tenille Jackson *(643-7589)*
James Jones *(643-6421)*
Valerie Kaskovich *(643-6439)*
Lamont Marner *(643-5729)*
Mike Ross *(643-3990)*
Tammy Smith *(643-2894)*
Tony Thiel *(643-2098)*
Sammy Thorn *(643-4286)*
Grace Tonies *(643-6376)*
Amy Turner *(643-2175)*
Joshua White *(643-3757)*
Anna Zilwaski *(643 2556)*

Damon Burns
Kasey Dasko
Nancy Decker
Rose Demont
Scott Floyd
Tenille Jackson
James Jones
Lamont Marner
Antonia Martinez
Sara Mauss
Tammy Smith
Jennifer Stanley
Tony Thiel
Sammy Thorn
J. C. Tucker
Amy Turner

The Lost Backpack
A Book Clue

We made a list of nine people who were on the soccer team and also in the summer reading program. We wrote down their names and phone numbers.

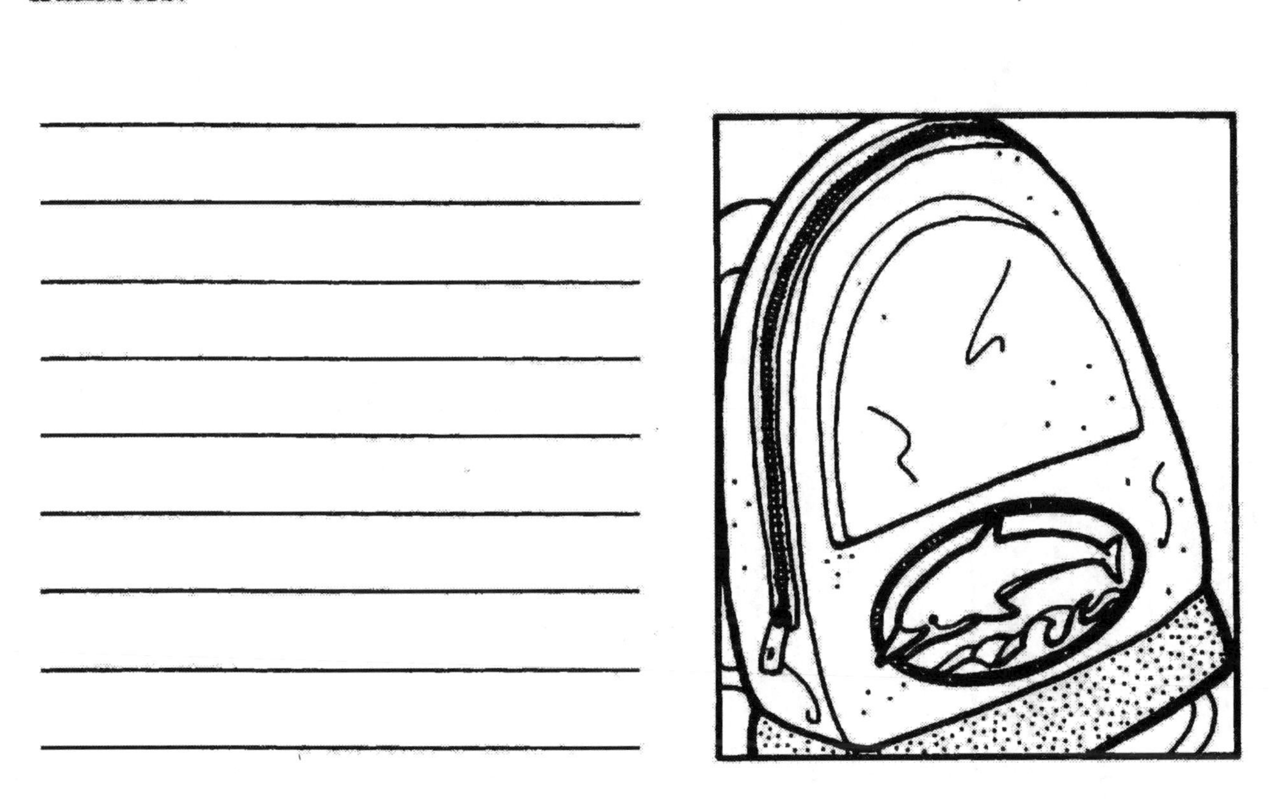

We still had a long way to go before we could find the owner of the backpack. That's when Sam's genius kicked in.

"The backpack has a neat picture of a dolphin on it. Maybe this means that the person really likes dolphins."

Digging books out of the bag, Sam exclaimed, "Look at these books! They are all about dolphins! If we knew which of the nine people likes books about dolphins, that could help us find out who the backpack belongs to."

Luckily, Jessica's mother had a file of the registration cards that the students had filled out for the summer reading program. The first question on the card asked what types of books the children liked to read.

"Sam, you're a genius," I said as I began pulling out the registration cards of the nine people on our list.

The Lost Backpack

A Book Clue, continued

Look at these nine registration cards. Circle the ones you think might have checked out books about dolphins.

SUMMER READING PROGRAM
Name: *Damon Burns*
List 3 types of books you like to read:
reptiles
baseball
sports heroes

SUMMER READING PROGRAM
Name: *Sammy Thorn*
List 3 types of books you like to read:
action adventure
race cars
water animals

SUMMER READING PROGRAM
Name: *Lamont Marner*
List 3 types of books you like to read:
dinosaurs
snakes
fishing

SUMMER READING PROGRAM
Name: *Amy Turner*
List 3 types of books you like to read:
animals
mysteries
arts and crafts

SUMMER READING PROGRAM
Name: *Tenille Jackson*
List 3 types of books you like to read:
planets
magic
drawing

SUMMER READING PROGRAM
Name: *Tony Thiel*
List 3 types of books you like to read:
ocean life
dog stories
science fiction

SUMMER READING PROGRAM
Name: *Rosa Demont*
List 3 types of books you like to read:
dinosaurs
soccer
girls in sports

SUMMER READING PROGRAM
Name: *Tammy Smith*
List 3 types of books you like to read:
mysteries
marine science
riddles and jokes

SUMMER READING PROGRAM
Name: *James Jones*
List 3 types of books you like to read:
mammals
insects
scary stories

The Lost Backpack

The Final Clue

Now we had narrowed the list to five people who were on the soccer team, were enrolled in the summer reading program and might have checked out books on dolphins. I made a list of the names and phone numbers of the five people.

______________________________ ______________________________

______________________________ ______________________________

____

When Sam started to put all of the books back in the backpack, he noticed a card in the bottom of the pack. The card was crumpled up and hard to read, but we could make out some writing on it.

"Look," he called as he held up the card. "Here's the final clue!"

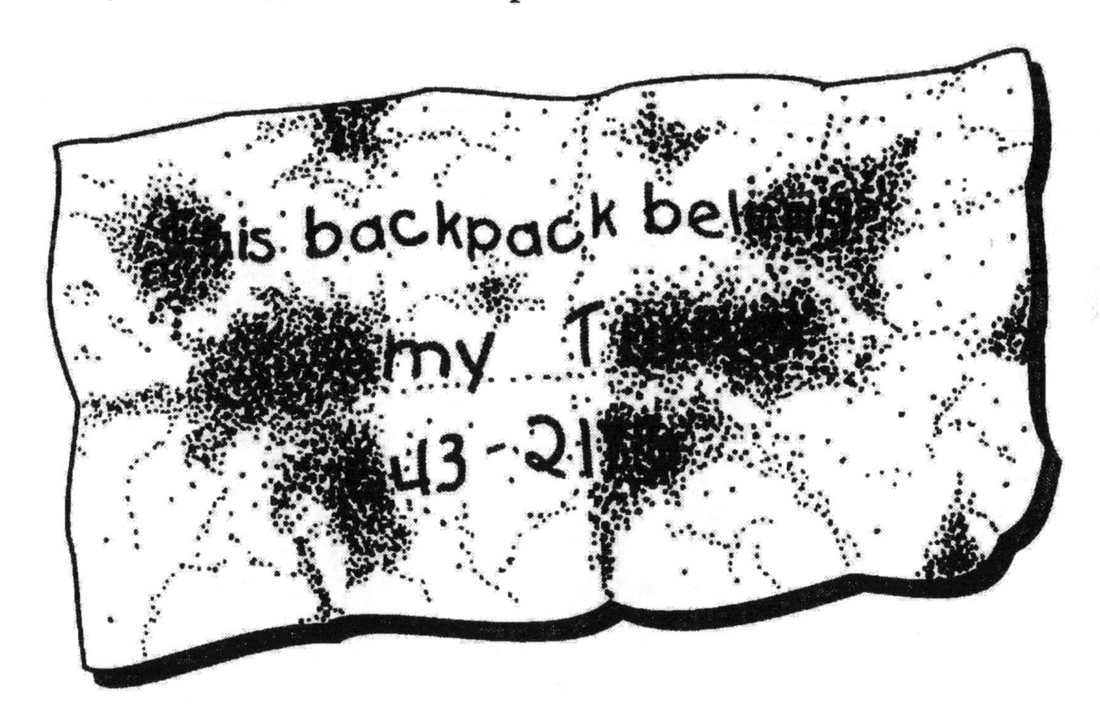

After comparing the card with the names and telephone numbers of the five people on our list, we knew who the backpack belonged to.

"Another case successfully solved," I declared. "The back pack belongs to ______________________________ **(fill in the owner's name).**

The Lost Backpack

Teacher's Guide

Two soccer players found a lost backpack, but it didn't have a name on it so they could return it to the owner. In this mystery, students need to analyze a variety of information and use a process of elimination to find the most likely owner of the lost backpack.

1. Discuss how we might go about finding the owner if we found a lost backpack. After reading over the scenario on page 27, discuss the logic of Rita's conclusion that the backpack belonged to someone on their soccer team who was also enrolled in the Super Summer Reading Program.
2. Point out to students that the names on page 28 are listed in alphabetical order according to last names. Crossing out names that can be found on only one list will help them find the ones that are on both lists. These names should be recorded on page 29.

   Names on both lists:

   Damon Burns
   Rose Demont
   Tenille Jackson
   James Jones
   Lamont Marner
   Tammy Smith
   Tony Thiel
   Sammy Thorn
   Amy Turner
3. Direct students to analyze the nine students' registration cards on page 30 and circle the names of people who might like books about dolphins.

   Answers:

   Sammy Thorn (water animals)
   Amy Turner (animals)
   Tony Thiel (ocean life)
   Tammy Smith (marine science)
   James Jones (mammals)
4. On page 31, have students list the five names and use the team roster to list their phone numbers. Have them analyze the writing on the card and compare it with the names and numbers on the list to determine the probable owner of the backpack.

   Answer:

   Amy Turner, phone 643-2175

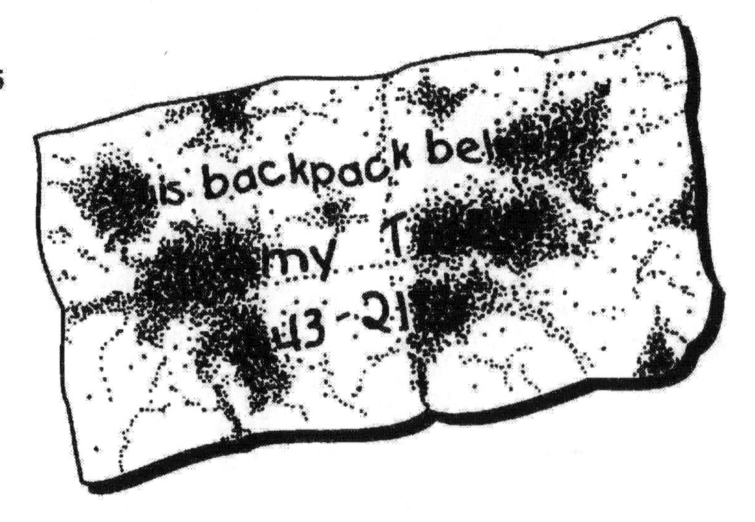

DOI: 10.4324/9781003234098-6

The Missing Ribbon

The Case

It was a warm spring day when the call from Mrs. Costello came in. She seemed quite upset, so even though we were in the middle of mixing up a batch of lemonade, Sam and I responded right away.

At the Sunnybrook School we found Mrs. Costello. She explained that all the boys in her class wanted to be the best at everything they did. This had caused many problems.

"But this last trick," she said as she shook her head, "is the worst thing that has happened so far. Lately, Jimmy seems to be winning at everything. The other boys are very jealous of Jimmy and all the attention he is getting."

"But this is no crime," we responded. "What is it you want us to do?"

"Well," she continued, "Jimmy's dog won first place in a dog show over the weekend. Jimmy brought in a picture of his dog and the first-place ribbon he won. I pinned the ribbon and picture up on the bulletin board. After recess, Jimmy discovered the ribbon was missing! He knew the other boys were jealous, and he thought one of them took the ribbon."

"Now we have a mystery," I whispered to Sam.

"Have no fear," I assured Mrs. Costello. "The Detective Club is on the trail of the ribbon robber. We'll have Jimmy's ribbon back in no time at all."

The Missing Ribbon

Making a Chart

Once we were alone, Sam and I decided that we should make a chart to keep track of all the information on the eight suspects Mrs. Costello had given us. I didn't know what information we would find, so I just made three columns. We decided we would fill in information as we uncovered clues.

Alex	________________	________________	________________
Tyler	________________	________________	________________
Matt	________________	________________	________________
Brett	________________	________________	________________
Jack	________________	________________	________________
Rahul	________________	________________	________________
Miguel	________________	________________	________________
Lee	________________	________________	________________

Save this chart. As you do the puzzles, fill in the clues about each person. When you have all the clues, complete these sentences.

The person who took the missing ribbon is ______________________________

He is the best suspect because ______________________________

____

The Missing Ribbon

Clues about Pets

Our first job was to talk to Jimmy. He told us that the missing ribbon said "First Place Dog Show." He thought maybe the person who took it also had a dog. That was at least a place to start. I put Sam on the pet detail while I went to investigate the crime scene. He quickly asked around and found clues about what pet each boy had. This is what he found out.

1. Jack's pet was an amphibian.
2. Tyler and Miguel had the same pet, but none of the other boys had that pet.
3. Matt's pet hopped.

Record the type of pet each person owned in the first column of the chart on page 35.

	newt	frog	cat	cat	dog	dog	dog	dog
Alex								
Tyler								
Matt								
Brett								
Jack								
Rahul								
Miguel								
Lee								

The Missing Ribbon
Recess Clues

Jimmy said his ribbon was on the bulletin board when he went out for morning recess. When he came in from recess, the ribbon was gone. He thought someone who had stayed in for recess must have taken his ribbon. I congratulated Jimmy on his sharp thinking and started to find out who might have stayed in for recess. As I questioned the other students I found the following clues.

1. Counting Jimmy, five of the boys in his class went out for recess.
2. The two boys with the same first initial played baseball together at recess, while Lee played on the swings.
3. The newt owner had to stay in to finish his math work, and Rahul stayed in to help him.
4. Both of the cat owners went out for recess.

I took my clues and found Sam. We were able to fill in another column in the chart. This one we labeled "recess" and wrote either "in" or "out" next to each name. What a team we were! We were going to easily crack this case.

Record this information in the second column of the chart on page 35.

The Missing Ribbon
Height Clues

When I was in the classroom I noted where the ribbon had been pinned. Some quick math calculations led me to the conclusion that the thief would have to be at least 51 inches tall to reach that high.

We asked Mrs. Costello for the heights of each suspect. She did not have a list of their heights, but she did give us this information.

1. Jack is the shortest boy in the class.
2. The tallest boy in the class has a dog.
3. Matt is 3 inches taller than Jack and 2 inches shorter than Lee.
4. Tyler is shorter than Brett, but he is 2 inches taller than Lee.
5. Rahul is taller than Alex, but he is shorter than Miguel.

All we had to do was record this information in the third column of our chart. Then we could give Mrs. Costello the name of the most likely suspect and close the case. Sam and I patted each other on the back. Another job well done!

Record this information in the third column of the chart on page 35.

1 / 2	46 inches	47 inches	48 inches	49 inches	51 inches	52 inches	53 inches	54 inches
Alex								
Tyler								
Matt								
Brett								
Jack								
Rahul								
Miguel								
Lee								

The Missing Ribbon

Teacher's Guide

Jealousy is the motive in the case of the missing ribbon. In this mystery, students will use matrix logic puzzles and analyze information about the boys in Jimmy's class to determine who is the most likely suspect to have taken his ribbon.

1. Introduce the scenario on page 34 and the chart on page 35 for students to fill in as they learn information about each of the other eight boys in Jimmy's class. Instruct them to fill in the information at the bottom of the page only after they have completed the chart. The chart is unlabeled. Students may label the first column "pet," second column "recess," and the third column "height" as they work through the puzzles.
2. Have students use the clues on page 36 to discover what pet each boy has. Label the first column of the chart "pet" and record the information on the chart.

   Answers:

Alex - dog	Jack - newt
Tyler - cat	Rahul - dog
Matt - frog	Miguel - cat
Brett - dog	Lee - dog

3. Have the students use the clues on page 37 along with the names on the chart to find who stayed in and who went out for recess. Record this information in the second column of the chart by labeling the column "recess" and writing "in" or "out" next to each name.
4. Give students the matrix logic puzzle on page 38 to determine each boys' height. Have them record the heights on their charts in the third column (which you will label "height") and then use the information in all three columns to decide whether or not each boy is a likely suspect. Record the name of the most likely suspect on the bottom of page 35.

   Answers:

Alex - 47 in.	Jack - 46 in.
Tyler - 53 in.	Rahul - 48 in.
Matt - 49 in.	Miguel - 52 in.
Brett - 54 in.	Lee - 51 in.

Answers:

Alex	dog	in	47 in.
Tyler	cat	out	53 in.
Matt	frog	out	49 in.
Brett	dog	in	54 in.
Jack	turtle	in	46 in.
Rahul	dog	in	48 in.
Miguel	cat	out	52 in.
Lee	dog	out	51 in.

Best Suspect: Brett (has a dog, stayed in for recess, and is over 51 inches tall.)

DOI: 10.4324/9781003234098-7

Willie's Wallet

The Case

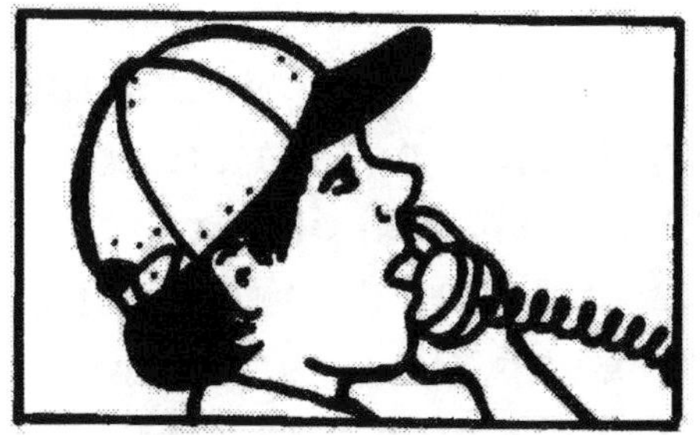

Summer vacation had just started and we were sitting around the club house talking about our summer plans. It wasn't too long, however, before our discussion was interrupted by a call from Mr. Corbin.

"We need some detectives to help find a missing wallet. Can you meet us at the carnival?"

This sounded like a case for quick thinkers, so we decided Sam Smart and Quent Quick should handle the case. They flew out the door. Rita and I went back to dreaming about summer.

Mr. Corbin met Sam and Quent at the carnival gate. With him was Willie, who looked very upset. Mr. Corbin explained that the Cub Scout pack had come to the carnival for an end-of-school celebration. Mr. Corbin divided the pack into three groups and assigned a father to each group. Willie was in Mr. Heider's group.

Sam and Quent were hurriedly taking notes as Mr. Corbin went on. "Each of the Cub Scouts was given tickets so he could ride on each of the five rides at the carnival. It wasn't until Willie got home that he discovered that his wallet was missing. He called me because I am the leader."

Sam and Quent could see that it might take a little time to get all the facts. Mr. Corbin was a man who liked to talk. So they interrupted him, "Just the facts please. We'll never find the wallet before the carnival closes tonight unless we get the facts and get busy."

Willie's Wallet
A Clue?

Mr. Corbin seemed intent on telling the whole story from the very beginning, so he continued, "The boys in all three groups started out at the carousel. Then the groups split up. All the groups went on the train, roller coaster, tilt-a-whirl, and octopus, but they rode the rides in a different order. We agreed everyone would go on the roller coaster last, because it was closest to the exit. Then each group would go home with the father who was in charge of the group."

"This could be a clue," Sam whispered to Quent. "We'll have to retrace Willie's steps."

"But," said Mr. Corbin, "I don't know in what order the groups rode the rides other than what they rode first and what they rode last."

"That's okay," Quent boasted and he pulled out a sharp pencil. "Sammy and I can figure it out." They quickly filled in a chart to show all the different ways the groups could have ridden the rides.

Fill in the chart with all the different ways the groups could have ridden on the five rides.

carousel	**2.**__________	**3.** __________	**4.**__________	roller coaster
carousel	**2.**__________	**3.** __________	**4.**__________	roller coaster
carousel	**2.**__________	**3.** __________	**4.**__________	roller coaster
carousel	**2.**__________	**3.** __________	**4.**__________	roller coaster
carousel	**2.**__________	**3.** __________	**4.**__________	roller coaster
carousel	**2.**__________	**3.** __________	**4.**__________	roller coaster

Willie's Wallet

Mapping the Route

Looking at the list of all the different ways the groups could have selected to go on the rides, Sam said, "I am not sure where this gets us."

Willie was too upset to be of much help, but he was able to give us a few clues about the rides his group rode on. He gave us these clues:

1. His group rode the tilt-a-whirl after the octopus
2. They rode the train after the tilt-a-whirl.

Put numbers by the rides to show the order in which Willie rode the rides.

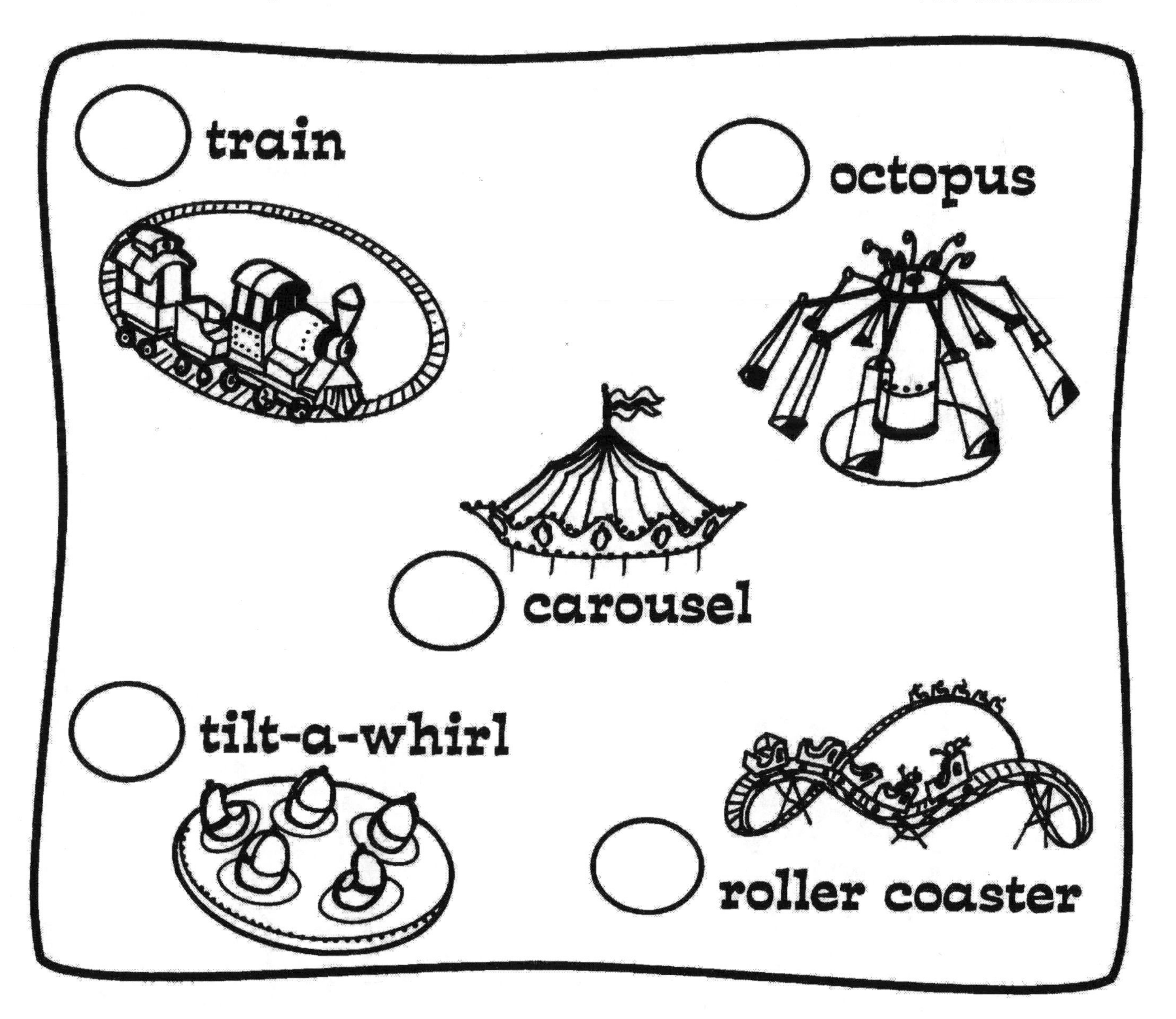

Willie's Wallet
The Wallet is Found

"You had the wallet when you started the rides and you discovered the wallet was missing when you got home, right?" said Sam.

Willie nodded yes.

"Then we'll just have to retrace your steps to see if we can find it at any of the other rides. We'll each check out one of the rides and meet at the second ride, the ______________________________ **(fill in the name)**."

When all four people met, they still had not located the wallet, but the operator of the second ride said that he had found it.

"I found the wallet and asked the people getting off the ride if it belonged to any of them. One boy said it wasn't his, but he thought it belonged to his friend Willie. I looked inside and saw Willie's name in the wallet, so I gave it to the boy to return to his friend," explained the operator.

"Who did you give it to?" asked Willie, finally daring to speak.

"I don't know his name, but he was wearing shorts, a black shirt, and a baseball cap," answered the operator.

Sam reasoned, "One of your friends must have taken your wallet, thinking he would give it to you later. Since the groups didn't meet after the last ride, he probably took it home. Someone who was in one of the two other groups has your wallet."

"Think about what everyone was wearing," I suggested to Mr. Corbin.

"Well, since it was a hot summer day, all the boys had on shorts," he said.

Underline the important clues that are given on this page.

Willie's Wallet

Cap Clues

"Then let's concentrate on hats," offered Quent, "Tell us everything you can remember about what kind of hats the boys in the other two groups were wearing. We'll have the wallet back in no time at all."

Willie and Mr. Corbin started scratching their heads, trying to remember all they could about the boys' hats. This is what they came up with.

1. The four boys in Mr. Corbin's group all wore hats.
2. The only boy in Mr. Todd's group to wear his Cub Scout cap was Sidney.
3. Sean and Craig wore the same kind of cap.
4. Trevor and Dameon both wore Chicago Cubs caps.

Mr. Todd's group				Mr. Corbin's group				
Leroy	Dameon	Troy	Sidney	Craig	Rick	Trevor	Sean	
								baseball cap
								baseball cap
								baseball cap
								Cub Scout cap
								Cub Scout cap
								Cub Scout cap
								no hat
								no hat

Willie's Wallet

Shirt Clues

"Now we're getting somewhere!" exclaimed Sam. Sam was always happy when he was making progress in a case. "Now," he continued, "tell us everything you can remember about what kind of shirt each boy wore."

This is what Willie and Mr. Corbin remembered.

1. Rick and Troy wore the same color shirts.
2. The color of Craig's shirt started with a vowel.
3. The color of Sidney's shirt had the same number of letters as his name.
4. Sean did not wear red, and Trevor did not wear black.
5. Dameon and Trevor wore the same color shirts.

		white	white	blue	yellow	orange	red	black	black
Mr. Corbin's group	Sean								
	Trevor								
	Rick								
	Craig								
Mr. Todd's group	Sidney								
	Troy								
	Dameon								
	Leroy								

Sam was really excited now. "That does it! That does it!" he screamed. "We know who has your wallet. ______________________ **(fill in the name)** has your wallet. Give him a call and I'm sure you'll find that he took your wallet home and planned to give it to you later."

Willie's Wallet
Teacher's Guide

What do you do when you have lost your wallet in a public place? You call the Detective Club. In this mystery, students have to gather information about the sequence in which Willie visited different rides and use deductive logic to determine which of his friends has his wallet.

1. Introduce the scenario of the Cub Scouts' trip to the carnival and the problem of Willie losing his wallet (page 41).

2. Have students list all of the possible routes the groups could take (starting with the carousel and ending with the roller coaster) on page 42.
   Answer:
   octopus - tilt-a-whirl - train
   octopus - train - tilt-a-whirl
   tilt-a-whirl - octopus - train
   tilt-a-whirl - train - octopus
   train - octopus - tilt-a-whirl
   train - tilt-a-whirl - octopus

3. On page 43, discuss Willie's problem, and the logic of retracing your steps to look for a missing belonging. Figure out the order of the rides for Willie's group and mark the route on the map.
   Answer:
   1. carousel 2. octopus 3. tilt-a-whirl 4. train 5. roller coaster

4. Page 44 contatins most dialogue about finding the wallet, but some important clues are given. Students sould underline the three clues that are given by the operator of the octopus.
   Answer:
   shorts, black shirt and baseball cap

5. Direct students to use the matrix on page 45 to solve the logic puzzle and find who wore caps that day, and what kind of cap each boy wore.
   Answers:
   baseball caps - Trevor, Rick and Dameon
   Cup Scout caps - Sean, Craig, and Sidney
   no caps - Troy and Leroy

6. Direct students to use the matrix on page 46 to solve the logic puzzle and find what color shirt each of the boys was wearing.
   Answers:

Sean - blue	Sidney - yellow
Trevor - white	Troy - black
Rick - black	Dameon - white
Craig - orange	Leroy - red

Answer
The boy that fits the description is **Rick** (baseball cap and black shirt.)

DOI: 10.4324/9781003234098-8

The Boys Only Club
The Case

Our friend Chuck came huffing and puffing into our office one day. He waved his hands frantically as he told us he had a horrible problem involving his birthday cake.

"Just start at the beginning, Chuck," I said smartly.

"Well, Shirley," he said, "there are six girls and four boys who live on Groton Lane. We all played together during summer vacation and usually got along quite well. When school started, the boys decided to have a 'Boys Only Club'. The girls really did not like being left out."

Quent and Sam nodded their heads in agreement. Rita and I shook our heads in disapproval.

"Well," continued Chuck, "each week one of the boys brings snacks to share. Today is my birthday. My mom baked a special birthday cake for the meeting. When I got home from school at 3:40 p.m., I took the cake and put it on the table in the tree house. Then I went in the house to wait for the other boys to arrive at 4:00 p.m. When they arrived, we all climbed up to the tree house, but the cake was gone!"

We all shared a look of shock.

"I am sure it was one of the girls getting even with us for not letting girls in our club, but I can't prove it. You have to help me find the cake."

Sam and Quent said they thought the girls had to be the guilty ones. Rita and I said we thought it was wrong to assume that the girls were guilty. So to give a fair hearing to both the girls and boys, we decided that a boy and a girl would take the case. I assigned Rita Right and Quent Quick.

The Boys Only Club

A Chart for Evidence

Quent said they had to start with the most likely suspects, who were, in fact, the girls in the neighborhood. If none of the girls were guilty, they would move on to other suspects.

Rita reluctantly agreed. They made a chart with the six girls' names on it and three columns to record information they found. Then they were on their way to Groton Street to find the missing birthday cake and return it to its owner.

As you get clues about the girls, record them on this chart.

Joan	____________	____________	____________
Sue	____________	____________	____________
Nikki	____________	____________	____________
Sally	____________	____________	____________
Dawn	____________	____________	____________
Jenny	____________	____________	____________

After you have all the clues, answer these questions:

Who is the most likely suspect? ______________________________

Why? ____

The Boys Only Club

A Clue About Time

Quent and Rita reasoned that the person who took the cake would have been in the neighborhood when the cake vanished, between 3:40 and 4:00 p.m. They questioned the neighbors about when each girl got home. They wrote down the clues and then used them to figure out when each girl arrived home.

?	3:40	3:45	3:45	3:50	4:15	4:45
Joan						
Sue						
Nikki						
Sally						
Dawn						
Jenny						

1. Sue's piano lesson lasted until 4:30 p.m.
2. Sally arrived home before Joan.
3. Joan and Dawn got home an hour before Sue.
4. Jenny arrived home later than Dawn.
5. Joan and Jenny got home after Sally but before Nikki.

Record the time each girl got home in the first column of the chart on page 50.

The Boys Only Club

Clues About Hair Color

Quent and Rita hot-footed it around the neighborhood looking for more clues. They found the lady who lived next door to Chuck and asked her if she had seen anyone near the tree house after school.

She recalled, "I saw a girl climbing down from the tree house. The girl had brown hair and was wearing blue jeans and a blue jacket."

"We have to find out what color hair each girl has and what each girl was wearing," said Rita. "Quent, you check out half the girls and I'll find out about the other half of the girls."

When Rita and Quent met, they had the following notes about the girls' hair colors.

1. Joan and Jenny had the same hair color.
2. Sue did not have brown hair.
3. Sue, Sally, and Dawn lived across the street from the red head.
4. Sally's hair was a lighter color than Dawn's hair.

Record the girls' hair colors in the second column of the chart on page 50.

	brown	brown	brown	blond	blond	red
Joan						
Sue						
Nikki						
Sally						
Dawn						
Jenny						

The Boys Only Club

Clues About Clothes

Now they just had to find out who was wearing blue jeans and a blue jacket and the case would be closed. Both Rita and Quent reported that all the girls they were trailing were wearing jeans.

"So," said Quent, "we just have to find out who was wearing a blue jacket. Let's write down what we found out about what each girl was wearing. Then we can figure out who stole the cake."

Quent and Rita wrote down what they knew about what each girl was wearing that day. Use the clues to find out what color jacket each girl wore.

1. None of the other girls had a jacket the same color as Sally's.
2. The girl with the red jacket walked to school every day with Sally, Joan, and the girl with the brown jacket.
3. The girl with the brown jacket lived next door to Dawn.
4. Nikki's mother drove her to school on her way to work every morning.
5. Sue rode her bike to school.

Write the color of each girl's jacket in the third column of the chart on page 50. Then write the name of the girl who took the cake.

	blue	blue	blue	black	red	brown
Joan						
Sue						
Nikki						
Sally						
Dawn						
Jenny						

The Boys Only Club

Teacher's Guide

In this mystery, students will use matrix logic puzzles to gain information about the six girls who are the suspects in the case. As they find information about each of the girls, they will record it on the chart. Analyzing the information on the chart will then lead them to the most likely suspect.

1. After reading the scenario on page 49, introduce the chart on page 50 for students to fill in as they learn information about each of the six girls. Instruct them to fill in the information at the bottom of the page after they have completed the chart. The chart is unlabeled. Students may label the first column "time," and second column "hair," the third column "blue jacket" as they work through the puzzles.
2. Have students use the clues on page 51 to find what time each of the girls got home from school and record the information in the first column on their charts.

   Answers:

Joan - 3:45	Sally - 3:40	Sue - 4:45
Dawn - 3:45	Nikki - 4:15	Jenny - 3:50

3. Have the students use the clues on page 52 to find what color hair each girl had and record the information in the second column of their charts.

   Answers:

Joan - brown	Sally - blond	Sue - blond
Dawn - brown	Nikki - red	Jenny - brown

4. Have the students use the clues on page 53 to find what color jacket each girl had and record the information in the third column of their charts.

   Answers:

Joan - blue	Sally - black	Sue - blue
Dawn - red	Nikki - blue	Jenny - brown

5. After all the information is recorded in the chart on page 50, direct students to analyze the information and decide whether or not each girl is a likely suspect.

   Answer: Joan is the most likely suspect. She has brown hair, a blue jacket, and got home between 3:40 and 4:00 p.m.

Answers:

	time	hair	blue jacket
Joan	3:45	brown	Yes
Sue	4:45	blond	Yes
Nikki	4:15	red	Yes
Sally	3:40	blond	No
Dawn	3:45	brown	No
Jenny	3:50	brown	No

DOI: 10.4324/9781003234098-9

Santa's Gift List

The Case

We were sitting around on Christmas Eve talking about what gifts we hoped we would get for Christmas when Quent answered a knock at the door.

"Shirley, you better come here," he whispered. "It's Santa. He needs our help. Can you believe it? We have never worked for a famous person before."

I was in shock as I came to the door and introduced myself. "I'm Shirley Sharp. Won't you please come in?"

Santa came in and started to describe his problem. It was Christmas Eve and he was busy delivering the toys. When he took out his list to check what toys he should deliver to each child, a big gust of wind blew one of the lists and the map right out of his hand. The list he lost was for the five children who lived on the 500 block of Brentwood Lane.

Without his list and his map, he couldn't remember what the five children wanted for Christmas and he couldn't figure out where each house was located. He called his elves and had them read the notes he had taken before he started, but he needed someone who was familiar with the neighborhood to decipher the notes.

That's where we came in. "Sure," I said. "We are experts in figuring out clues. We can help you match up each gift with a person and a house. Just give us the information you have and we'll get to work on the case."

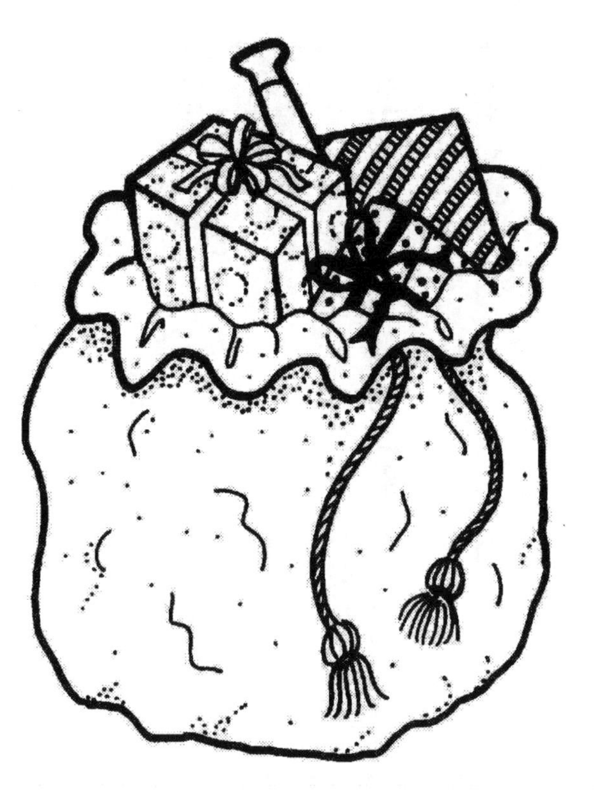

"Well," chuckled Santa, "the five gifts I have left in my pack are a magic kit, a Monopoly game, art supplies, a science kit, and a Lego set. And here is all the other information my elves gave me. It is kind of mixed up. While you work on the case, I'll just sit here and eat some of my cookies and drink some milk."

We immediately started sorting out clues and making a map of the 500 block of Brentwood Lane. We were sure we'd have this case finished before Santa could get to his third batch of cookies, but it was a little harder than we expected. The information from the elves was more mixed up than we thought possible. Quent read the clues as the rest of us referred to a map of Brentwood Lane.

"This is very confusing. I can tell right away," said Quent, "that we will have to find out some more information about the houses before we can do anything with this information."

"We'll need all four of us on this case," I added. "Let's take a walk to Brentwood Lane and get some information about the houses. If Santa comes with us, there are enough people so that everyone can take one house."

"Let's go!" we shouted as we put on our coats. Santa reluctantly left his cookies and milk and followed us.

Santa's Gift List

The Houses on Brentwood Lane

This is the diagram we made of the houses on Brentwood Lane. We wrote information about the **color** and the **building materials** of the houses and the **first names** and **last names** of the children on each line.

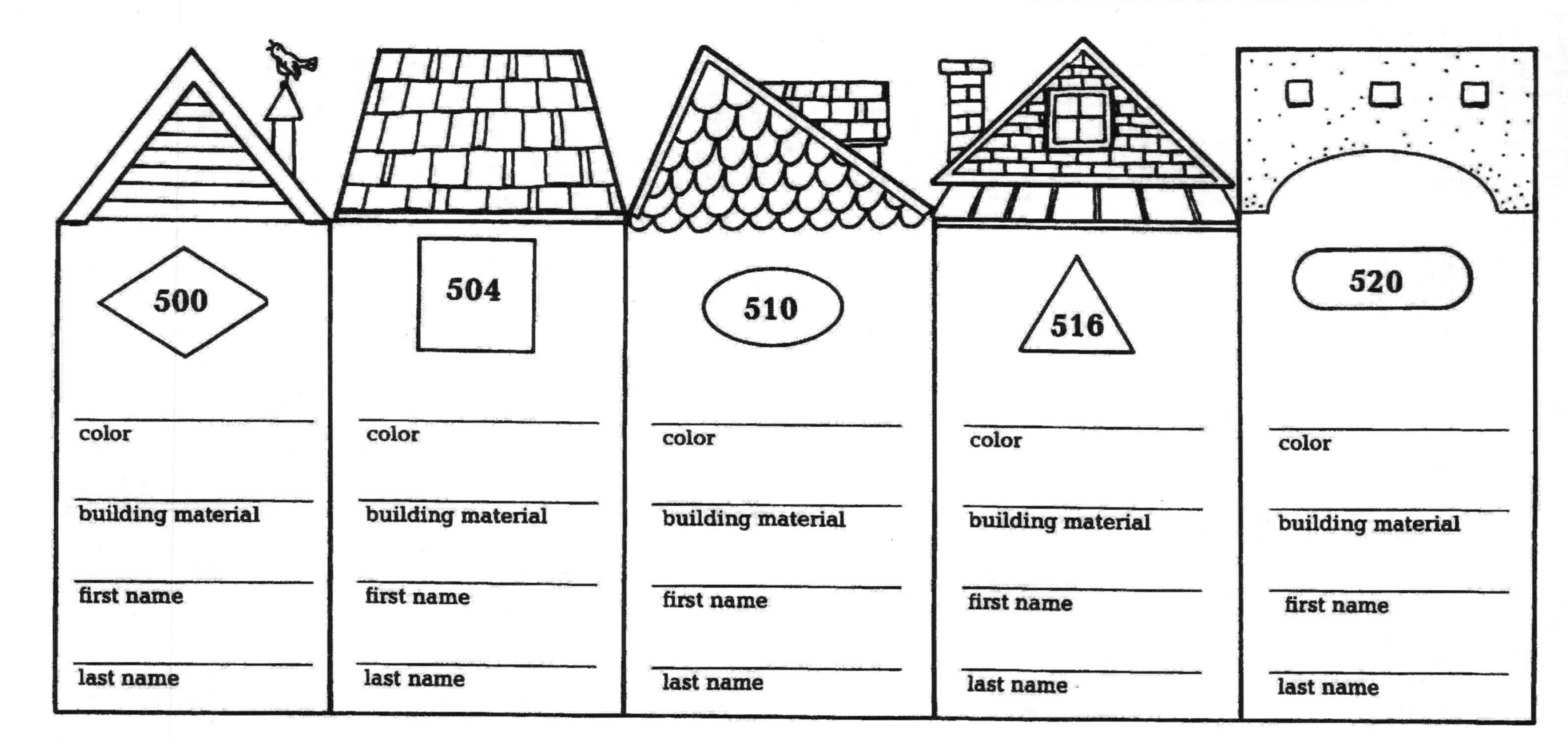

Santa's Gift List

Color of the Houses

When we surveyed the houses we found that there were five different colors. The houses were white, yellow, red, brown, and blue. The names of the children who lived in the houses were Jacob, Anja, Lauren, Sean, and Raja. This is what we found about the colors of the houses and the names of the children who lived in each house.

1. Lauren, Raja, and Anja lived in houses the colors of the American flag.
2. Anja and Sean lived next door to the yellow house.
3. The white house was between Lauren's and Anja's.
4. The address of the blue house was 510 Brentwood Lane.
5. Lauren's house had the lowest number address.

Put this information on the first and third lines of the diagram of houses on page 58.

Santa's Gift List
Building Materials

"We're part way there," I told my team. "Now we have to figure out the rest of the information about the houses. What did we find out about the houses' building materials?"

"We found out that the houses were made of bricks, stucco, wood siding, aluminum siding, and shingles," said Sam. "Let's sort out this information."

1. The brick house was built with red bricks.
2. The house with the wood siding was between Anja's house and Sean's houses.
3. The house with shingles was between Raja's house and Jacob's house.
4. The address of the stucco house was 520 Brentwood Lane.

Put this information on the second line of the diagram of the houses on page 58.

Santa's Gift List

Last Names

"And one more thing," said Santa. "I would really like to know the last names of the children so I can check them off the list when I get back. I know that the last names of the children are Riley, Moran, Seitner, Cohen, and Solanka, but I don't know which last name goes with which first name. Can you figure this out if I give you some more information?"

We were getting tired and hungry, but we all agreed to help him figure out this one last piece of the puzzle.

"This one is tough," said Rita. "We'll have to use the information we have filled in on our diagram of the houses along with these clues Santa gave us.

1. Anja and Raja had last names that begin with S.
2. Cohen lived between Seitner and Sean.
3. Raja lived between Lauren and Seitner.
4. Moran's house address was a lower number than Solanka's.

Put this information on the fourth line of the diagram of the houses on page 58.

Santa's Gift List

The Case is Closed

We had finished recording all the information about the five houses and the kids who lived there. We checked the notes from the elves that told who got what gift. The clues were easy to decode now that we knew who lived in each house.

1. The Lego set belonged at the house with the shingles.
2. The Monopoly game went to the house with the lowest address.
3. The art supplies belonged in the house between the red and blue houses.
4. The child who lived at 520 Brentwood Lane got the science kit.
5. The magic kit needed to go in the house next to the stucco house.

Write the name of the child who should receive each gift.

Lego set - ____________________ **Monopoly game -**____________________

art supplies - ____________________ **magic kit -** ____________________

science kit - ____________________

"There you go Santa," I said. "Your mystery is solved. You can now deliver the correct gifts to the children."

In a wink of the eye, he was gone to finish his rounds. He left us all his cookies and milk and a detective kit.

"What a guy!" we all said together.

Santa's Gift List
Teacher's Guide

It's rare that Shirley and her fellow detectives get a famous client, but it happened one Christmas Eve. In this case students have to sort through information about five houses and the people who live in the houses, so they can help Santa determine who gets what gift. This is a very difficult mystery in that students have to combine information from several different exercises onto one chart. Give this mystery to students only after they are very familiar with the whole process of solving the mysteries in this book.

1. Read the introduction on page 56 and 57. Explain that they will be given clues to help them find out who lives in each house. Once they have this information, they will be asked to match up all the information and determine who gets what gift.
2. Introduce the diagram of the five houses on page 58. Point out the house numbers ranging from 500 to 520 Brentwood Lane. Explain to the students that as they find information about the houses and who lives in them, they should fill in the blanks inside the houses. When the chart is complete, line 1 will have the color of the house, line 2 the building material of the house, line 3 the first name of the child who lives there, and line 4 the last name.
3. Direct students to use the clues on page 59 to find the color of each child's house. Instruct them to use the information in the clues to fill in the house colors on line 1 of their diagram and the first names of the children on line 3.

   Answers: (lines 1 and 3)

	500	**504**	**510**	**516**	**520**
line 1	red	white	blue	yellow	brown
line 3	Lauren	Raja	Anja	Jacob	Sean

4. Direct students to use the information they have written on their diagram along with the clues on page 60 to find the building material of each house. Instruct them to write the building material on line 2 of the diagram.

   Answers: (line 2)

500	**504**	**510**	**516**	**520**
brick	aluminum siding	shingles	wood siding	stucco

5. Have students use the clues on page 61 to find each child's last name. The last names should be written on line 4, completing the diagram.

   Answers: (line 4)

500	**504**	**510**	**516**	**520**
Moran	Solanka	Seitner	Cohen	Riley

6. Direct students to find out who should receive each gift by using the information on their completed diagram and the clues on page 62. They should record this information on the bottom of page 62.

Answers:

Lego set - Anja Seitner
art supplies - Raja Solanka
magic kit - Jacob Cohen
Monopoly game - Lauren Moran
science kit - Sean Riley

SUPER DETECTIVE

CERTIFICATE

This is to certify that

____

has successfully solved

____

mysteries and is entitled
to be a detective with
The Detective Club.

Congratulations on a job well done.

________________ ________________

date signed

Common Core State Standards Alignment Sheet

Detective Club

All lessons in this book align to the following standards.

Grade Level	Common Core State Standards in ELA-Literacy
Grade 2	RF.2.3 Know and apply grade-level phonics and word analysis skills in decoding words RF.2.4 Read with sufficient accuracy and fluency to support comprehension.
Grade 3	RF.3.3 Know and apply grade-level phonics and word analysis skills in decoding words RF.3.4 Read with sufficient accuracy and fluency to support comprehension.
Grade 4	RF.4.3 Know and apply grade-level phonics and word analysis skills in decoding words RF.4.4 Read with sufficient accuracy and fluency to support comprehension.

Printed in the United States
by Baker & Taylor Publisher Services